THE WORLD AT WAR
WORLD WAR II

The Home Front

Heinemann
LIBRARY

Brenda Williams

www.heinemann.co.uk/library
Visit our website to find out more information about **Heinemann Library** books.

To order:
 Phone 44 (0) 1865 888066
Send a fax to 44 (0) 1865 314091
 Visit the Heinemann Bookshop at www.heinemann.co.uk/library to browse our catalogue and order online.

First published in Great Britain by Heinemann Library, Halley Court, Jordan Hill, Oxford OX2 8EJ, part of Harcourt Education.
Heinemann is a registered trademark of Harcourt Education Ltd.

Editorial: Andrew Farrow and Dan Nunn
Design: Lucy Owen and Tokay Interactive Ltd
 (www.tokay.co.uk)
Picture Research: Hannah Taylor and Sally
 Claxton
Production: Victoria Fitzgerald

Originated by Repro Multi Warna
Printed and bound China by
WKT Company Limited

The paper used to print this book comes from sustainable resources.
ISBN-13: 978 0 431 10377 8 (HB)
ISBN-10:   0 431 10377 1 (HB)
10 09 08 07 06
10 9 8 7 6 5 4 3 2

ISBN-13: 978 0 431 10384 6 (PB)
ISBN-10:   0 431 10384 4 (PB)
10 09 08 07
10 9 8 7 6 5 4 3 2 1

British Library Cataloguing in Publication Data
Williams, Brenda, 1946–
 The Home Front. – (World at war. World War II)
 1. World War, 1939–1945 – Social aspects – Great Britain – Juvenile literature 2. Great Britain – History – George VI, 1936–1952 – Juvenile literature
 I. Title
 941'.084
A full catalogue record for this book is available from the British Library.

Acknowledgements
The publishers would like to thank the following for permission to reproduce photographs:

Australian War Memorial p. **27 top**; Corbis pp. **4** (Hulton Deutsch Collection), **5** (Bettmann), **6 right** (Bettmann), **8** (Hulton Deutsch Collection), **9** (Hulton Deutsch Collection), **10**, **11 bottom** (Bettmann), **11 top** (Hulton Deutsch Collection), **13** (Bettmann), **14** (Hulton Deutsch Collection), **17** (Hulton Deutsch Collection), **20**, **23 bottom** (Hulton Deutsch Collection), **24** (Hulton Deutsch Collection), **25** (Hulton Deutsch Collection), **26** (Bettmann), **27 bottom** (Bettmann), **28** (Bettmann); Getty Images pp. **15 bottom** (Hulton Archive), **16** (Hulton Archive), **18 bottom** (Hulton Archive), **19 bottom** (Hulton Archive), **19 top** (Time Life Pictures), **21** (Hulton Archive), **22** (Hulton Archive); Imperial War Museum pp. **7**, **23 top**; Topfoto.co.uk pp. **6 left** (The Lord Price Collection), **12** (LAPI/Roger Viollet), **15 top** (Roger Viollet), **18 top** (Public Record Office/HIP).

Cover photograph of a family fitting their gas-masks reproduced with permission of Topham Picturepoint.

Every effort has been made to contact copyright holders of any material reproduced in this book. Any omissions will be rectified in subsequent printings if notice is given to the publishers.

CONTENTS

Some words are shown in bold, **like this**. You can find out what they mean by looking in the glossary.

THE HOME FRONT

In most wars, armies fight along battle fronts, lines where the two sides meet. In World War II (1939–1945) there was also a Home Front, because people in every home in every country at war were affected.

A worldwide war

World War II began in Europe. On 1 September 1939, German armies invaded Poland. Two days later, Britain and France, followed by allies such as Australia and Canada, declared war on Germany. On 7 December 1941, Japan attacked the US naval base at Pearl Harbor in Hawaii. This brought the United States into the war.

In this global war, millions of people suffered invasion and **occupation**. This happened to the people of China, Poland, Czechoslovakia, the USSR, Norway, Holland, France, Greece, the Philippines, and many other countries. Their villages and cities became battle zones. Families lost their homes and possessions. Millions of men, women, and children were killed or injured. In some countries, **civilian** deaths far outnumbered military **casualties**.

▼ In World War II, armies moved at speed across countries, backed up by aircraft. These German troops are pictured advancing through Poland in 1939. As the invaders swept through towns and villages, many civilians were killed or forced to flee.

Britain was not invaded, but its people lived through five years of bombing. For people in Australia, Canada, and the United States too, the war brought shortages, fears, and great changes in daily life. The "Home Front" involved everyone, young and old. As the years passed, and wartime rules became routine, people wondered: how long could it last? And would life ever be the same again?

1 September 1939	3 September 1939	April–May 1940
German armies invade Poland in a *Blitzkrieg* or "lightning war".	Britain and France go to war with Germany but cannot save Poland.	Germany invades first Denmark and Norway, then Belgium, Holland, and France. In June, Italy joins the war on the side of Germany.

▲ Bombing from the air added to civilians' misery. These people in London tried to save what they could from the ruins of their wrecked homes.

Eyewitness

In Britain, Doreen Atkinson remembered her mother baking as the family listened to the radio news of war on 3 September 1939. Her uncles had been killed in World War I, 1914–1918.

"She stood with her floury hands half raised above the mixing bowl ... her eyes brimmed over. She had seen it all before and memories of her dead brothers came crowding in."

Estimate of deaths in World War II

Country	Military	Civilians
China	1,300,000	Unknown, up to 20 million?
France	213,000	350,000
Germany	3,500,000	780,000
Japan	1,300,000	672,000
Poland	123,000	5,600,000
Soviet Union	11,000,000	7,000,000
United Kingdom	264,000	93,000
United States	292,000	6,000

It is thought about 18 million members of the armed forces from all countries died fighting on land, sea, and in the air. There are no accurate figures for civilians, but it is estimated that twice as many may have died during the war.

17 June 1940
France stops fighting. Britain and its Commonwealth allies stand alone against Germany.

22 June 1941
Hitler orders German armies to invade the Soviet Union (Russia).

7 December 1941
Japanese naval planes attack the US base at Pearl Harbor, Hawaii. The United States is at war. Next day, Britain and its allies go to war with Japan too.

The build-up to war

The war was not a surprise to people around the world. For many years the **Nazi** leader Adolf Hitler had been building up Germany's armed forces. In 1938, Germany had taken over Austria and much of Czechoslovakia, to create a bigger German empire or *Reich*.

Hot news

People followed news about world events in newspapers and on the radio, and cinemas also showed news reports. In Germany, the Nazi government showed Hitler making speeches to thousands of people, and used the media to support its policies. In countries such as Britain, France, the United States, and Australia, governments tried to educate their people about the threat from Germany.

Preparing for war

Countries in Europe began to build up their armed forces. Even the United States, which did not expect to go to war in Europe, spent billions of dollars on new equipment. When war broke out in Europe, the United States supplied Britain and France, and later the Soviet Union, with arms and food.

▲ On 3 September 1939, two days after Hitler's attack on Poland, New York's evening papers carried news that France and Britain had declared war on Germany.

◀ Gas masks were issued by governments in case enemy planes dropped poison-gas bombs. No one liked wearing the rubber masks, but everyone had to carry one. There were even gas masks for horses!

◀ **Sandbags** were filled to be used as protection around buildings and shelter-trenches were dug in parks in case of **air raids**. In the autumn of 1939, children were also **evacuated** from London and other British cities to escape the bombs.

Eyewitness

In 1939, Leonora Pitt was a teenager in the English Midlands. She remembered, "When war was declared, Mum said 'God help us!' and cried. Dad said he knew it was coming."

Her brother decided to join the Royal Air Force.

"Me, at fourteen, I just felt excited."

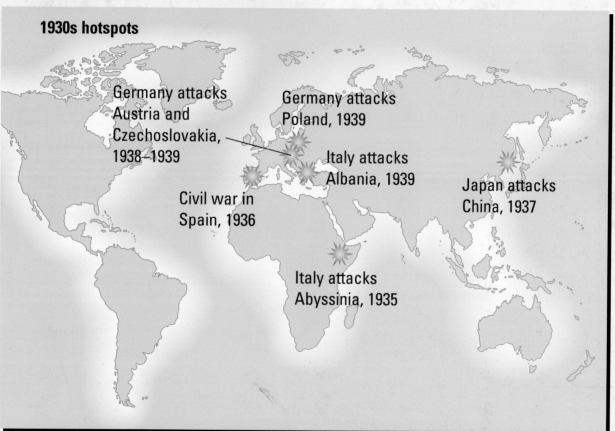

1930s hotspots

Germany attacks Austria and Czechoslovakia, 1938–1939

Germany attacks Poland, 1939

Italy attacks Albania, 1939

Civil war in Spain, 1936

Japan attacks China, 1937

Italy attacks Abyssinia, 1935

▲ In the 1930s, the news media reported trouble around the world. Dictators like Adolf Hitler used military power to get what they wanted. In the 1930s Germany, Italy, and Japan wanted more territory. Their aggression led the world to war.

LIFE IN WARTIME

In wartime, governments wanted people to live and work as normally as possible. Children went to school, and workers continued to go to their desks and factory benches. Even in 1940–1941, when Britain was bombed, the "war effort" had to go on.

In the United States and Canada, and in most of Australia, daily life went on much as before the war. But people had to work harder. Factories were ordered to increase production – more guns, more tanks, more boots, more of everything. People were sent to new jobs in war industries, and some jobs changed – for example, some factories that made wooden furniture changed to making aircraft. Everywhere there were government posters urging people to work for victory. Radio and newspapers carried war news every day.

Women at work

Family life changed too. Millions of women did war work, some going to work for the first time. By December 1943, women made up a third of Britain's engineering workforce. Yet unfairly, even when doing the same work, women were usually paid less than men. Millions of women with children combined a job with running a home, often alone since so many men were away on military service or war work.

▲ A female munitions (weapons) worker in a factory in 1940. Millions of women worked hard to keep factories running and supply all the weapons needed to win the war.

May 1940	17 June 1940	September 1940
In Britain, the working week in aircraft factories goes up, to 70 hours.	France is defeated, and northern France is occupied by German troops. French factories begin working for the German war effort.	After failing to defeat the RAF in the Battle of Britain, German bombers attack London and other British cities.

◀ Streets were often blocked by fallen buildings after an air raid. The ground was strewn with bricks, glass, shattered wood, and roof tiles. Going to work or school often meant a long walk because buses could not get through.

A war for everyone

The war affected everyone, young and old. Most people were **patriotic** and wanted their side to win, but everyone wanted the war to be over. Those who would not fight for moral reasons (called "conscientious objectors"), worked on farms or in hospitals. In wartime there were more rules, less freedom, and shortages – especially of food and fuel. Keeping clean wasn't easy: to save water, British people were asked to use no more than 5 inches (12.5 cm) of water in their baths. Everybody had to carry **identity cards** and needed ration books to buy food and clothes. During the **blackout** at night, windows had to be curtained over to stop any light showing. But even during the **Blitz** (the bombing of British cities) children still had to go to school!

In the News

A British "work harder" poster told readers "It's Your Personal War". The message was: "Your opposite number works fast ... you must beat him". One picture showed "Mr Coleman" in a British factory going home early, while in Nazi Germany "Mr Kaufmann" kept working hard. Another showed "Phyllis Brown" gossiping over a cup of tea, while "Paula Braun" worked non-stop (watched by a stern Nazi).

9

April–May 1941	December 1941	February 1943
First US ships with war food supplies reach Britain.	The British government can order people to do "essential war work". All women aged 20–30 must register for war work.	Germany calls up all men and women aged 16–65 for war work.

Schooling in wartime

The war did not stop education. Most children went to school, and took exams, even though many went straight into the armed forces after they left school. If a school was blown up or damaged, children and teachers moved to another building. Gas masks and air raid drills became part of classroom routine. Children hurried to the air raid shelter when the sirens sounded. Inside, safe from the bombs, they listened to stories, sang or did craft hobbies – or went on with the lesson – until the "all clear" signal. Then teachers and children went back to the classroom.

Some city children moved to new schools in the country. This could be exciting, though many children felt a bit homesick. Jewish children under Nazi rule in occupied countries were less fortunate. Most were forced to leave their schools. Millions of Jews, including many children, were sent to concentration camps – prisons holding thousands of captives. There they were worked to death or killed immediately.

Helping the war effort

Schoolchildren helped the war effort in various ways:

- they collected paper, glass, bones, and scrap metal for recycling

- they saved pocket money to help the war effort

- they saved food waste in bins to feed pigs

- they knitted hats, gloves, and scarves for soldiers and refugees

- they dug "victory gardens" to provide fresh vegetables.

▶ Children in the US capital, Washington, DC, collect scrap metal for the war effort.

◀ City children in Britain were evacuated by train and bus to the country. Some schools took over big country houses and summer camps. Country life came as a shock to children who were horrified to see milk coming from "smelly cows", not nice clean bottles!

In the News

"The schools and the teachers are in no sense outside the nation's war effort; they are right in it!"
British government leaflet:
The School in Wartime, 1941

▼ In September 1939, around 750,000 British schoolchildren were evacuated. By Christmas, most were settled into new schools. There was another mass evacuation in 1940, after the Blitz on Britain's cities began. It was important to be prepared for air raids: these children are sheltering under their desks.

Eyewitness

Most children soon got used to air raids. One British teacher was surprised after his school's first air raid:

"... the boys were rubbing their hands with glee in expectation of the bomb splinters and other souvenirs they would be able to collect."

LIVING BEHIND ENEMY LINES

For millions of people, the war meant living under enemy rule. Every day was a struggle – to find food, to keep warm, to stay alive.

Much of Europe was under Nazi rule from 1940 until 1945. In Asia, the Japanese took over much of China, Southeast Asia, Indonesia, and the Philippines. People in these occupied countries were often treated cruelly, living in fear of imprisonment or death. The occupiers took what they wanted: food, land, houses, farms, factories, even art treasures.

Collaborate or resist?

After France was defeated in 1940, half the country was governed by the Nazis. The rest, known as Vichy, was ruled by French officials who did what the Nazis told them. In France and other occupied countries, some people gave in and decided to help the invaders; they became **collaborators**. Others chose to fight on as members of the "underground" or secret **Resistance** army.

The plight of the Jews

The Nazis had begun to persecute German Jews before the war, and then took this race-hate across occupied Europe. They rounded up Jews and other peoples, such as Slavs and the Roma (gypsies) from across Poland, Holland, Russia, and other countries. Some Jewish communities were shut inside walled areas called **ghettos**. This happened in Warsaw, Poland's capital. Many more Jews were taken in trains to concentration camps.

▲ Millions of Europeans suffered under Nazi occupation. German soldiers patrolled the streets, stopping to check people's identity papers. Anyone suspected of helping the Resistance was shot or hanged.

September 1939	9 April 1940	May 1940
After the invasion of Poland, Nazis hunt down Jews and force Poles to work for the German war effort.	German troops invade Denmark and Norway. In Norway, Vidkun Quisling heads a government that supports Germany.	German armies invade Belgium, Luxembourg, Holland, and France. The British Channel Islands fall into enemy hands in June 1940.

▲ By 1942 the Nazis had begun systematically rounding up Jews. Some 6 million Jews were killed during World War II, about 4 million of them in **death-camps**. This mass slaughter became known as the **Holocaust**.

The terrors of occupation

- Starvation – the Nazis took most food for themselves.

- Curfew – people had to stay at home at night or risk being shot by the police.

- The Gestapo – the German security police could arrest anyone.

- Torture – many prisoners were tortured by the Gestapo.

- Travel problems – people could not even visit the next town without permission.

- Censorship – the Nazis controlled all media. Listening to Allied radio (such as the BBC) was a crime.

- Being spied on – collaborators "told tales" on their neighbours.

Eyewitness

Cornelia Fuykschot was twelve in May 1940 when the Netherlands was invaded. Her parents were listening in horror to the early morning radio news: "Parachutists have landed!" She remembered her father's grim voice "This is war", while her mother calmly said "Let's have breakfast", knowing that life had to carry on, somehow. Not until 1945 would the Dutch people be free.

6 April 1941
Yugoslavia and Greece are invaded by Germany. Partisans (resistance groups) fight back.

22 June 1941
Germany invades the Soviet Union. Millions of Russians are killed.

January–May 1942
The Japanese conquer Malaya, Singapore, the Dutch East Indies, and the Philippines.

Resistance fighters

Resistance groups in occupied countries such as France and the Netherlands formed an "underground" secret army. Sometimes Resistance bands fought gun-battles with enemy troops, but more often they used **sabotage** – wrecking factory machines or blowing up railways.

Allied agents were trained in spying and secret warfare. They landed in occupied countries by parachute, plane, or submarine to help the Resistance. It was very dangerous. Anyone caught by the German security police, the Gestapo, faced almost certain death. The Gestapo also retaliated cruelly – for every one German killed by the Resistance, they would kill perhaps ten local people.

Eyewitness

Lise de Baissac was a French secret agent, working for the British **Special Operations Executive (SOE)**. In September 1942, she was parachuted into France, and took a flat in the town of Poitiers – next door to the Gestapo headquarters. "I was very lonely," she remembered, because "Having false papers, I never received a letter or a telephone call." She returned to England in 1943, but was back in France in April 1944, carrying guns and explosives for sabotage missions. Lise de Baissac survived the war and died in 2004, aged 98.

▼ Men and women with jobs in factories, garages, schools, and shops risked their lives to work and fight for the Resistance.

LIVING BEHIND ENEMY LINES

Warsaw uprising

500,000 Polish Jews were prisoners in the Warsaw ghetto. Most were starving and sick. In 1942, the Nazis began removing 5,000 people a day. They took them to the gas chambers. In April 1943, 1,500 resistance fighters led by Mordechai Anielewicz fought the Nazis for three weeks. All but 80 Jews were killed in this Warsaw Rising. Anielewicz, along with others, killed himself rather than be captured.

▲ German soldiers in Warsaw, the centre of Polish resistance to the Nazis. The Jewish uprising of 1943 was brutally crushed.

Resistance tactics

- Each Resistance group had its own network of fighters and helpers.
- "Safe houses" were used as hiding places.
- Couriers rode bicycles from town to town with secret messages.
- Agents hid radios in suitcases or under floorboards.
- Resistance groups smuggled shot-down Allied airmen to safety.

▲ Members of the French Resistance study weapons dropped by parachute into Nazi-occupied France.

NATIONS HOLD ON

NATIONS HOLD ON

In countries at war, public services still had to be kept going, despite damage to roads, railways, and factories. Governments urged people to support the war effort.

Keeping on the move

People had to get to their war work every day, and night too. Very few people in Europe had their own cars, and anyway there was hardly any petrol because of fuel rationing. So it was important to keep buses and trains moving. Railways and ports were vital to keep food and war supplies flowing. After every air raid, city workers repaired smashed water and gas pipes, and reconnected electricity supplies.

▲ Listening to the "wireless". Allied leaders Winston Churchill and Franklin D Roosevelt spoke to their people on the radio. So did Hitler in Germany.

Firefighters fought blazes started by incendiary (fire) bombs and rescuers dug out people trapped beneath collapsed buildings. Cinemas and theatres, closed at the start of war, soon reopened. So did restaurants, even when there was little on the menu because of food rationing.

The media war

There was a **propaganda** war as well as fighting. In Germany, Joseph Goebbels made sure that films, radio, newspapers, and posters put across the Nazi view of the war. Broadcasts from Germany by William Joyce, a Briton working for the Nazis, were intended to weaken Britain's will to fight. But most British people thought Joyce, nicknamed "Lord Haw-Haw", was a joke. They preferred to believe Winston Churchill. In June 1940 he told them, "we shall fight on the beaches … we shall never surrender". Radio and newspapers spread the war messages. Posters urged people to work harder, talk less, turn off the light, walk to work, and plant vegetables!

16

March 1940	1 July 1940	8 December 1941
Professional soccer re-starts in Britain. Sport is good for public morale and crowds soon pack the soccer grounds.	The British government announces that phone links to the Channel Islands have been cut – Germany has invaded the islands.	Broadcasting to Americans, President Roosevelt speaks of a "date that will live in infamy" after Japan attacks Pearl Harbor.

Typical wartime slogans:

We can't win without them
Poster encouraging women to work (USA)

Walk when you can
Poster urging people not to use vehicles whenever possible (Britain)

Blackout means black
Reminding people to shut curtains and blinds at night (USA)

Keep mum – the world has ears
Warning people not to gossip in case spies are listening (USA)

If THEY starve WE starve
Asking people to save food scraps for farm animals (Britain)

Eyewitness

"Things got more difficult as the months went by. Water and gas got cut off due to bombed gas and water mains. Industry was disrupted with electricity cuts. Permanent waves [hair-curling using electric curlers] were a hazard ... a power-cut left you wet, cold, and with half a perm."

Leonora Pitt, from Walsall, England. She worked in an iron foundry with her grandfather, father, uncle, and brother.

▲ Repair gangs worked constantly to keep Britain's railways, water mains, telephone cables, and other essential services running through the Blitz.

March–April 1942

British bombers target the German port of Lübeck. In retaliation, German planes bomb British towns such as Exeter, Bath, Norwich, and York.

April 1942

Japan experiences a US air raid for the first time. American B-25 bombers launched from an aircraft carrier attack Tokyo.

January 1944

German factories are hit hard by Allied bombing. The Nazis order all children over ten to do war work.

Digging for victory

Governments sent out millions of leaflets, telling people how they could help to win the war. One way was to grow more food. In Britain many foods were rationed, so a poster showing a basket brimming with tasty vegetables caught the eye: the message was "Your own vegetables all the year round … if you DIG for Victory NOW". In the United States, a government poster showed a tractor on a farm, leading tanks and aircraft. Its message, "Food Comes First", emphasized how important food was to the war effort.

Gardeners and Land Girls

Books and newspaper articles showed new gardeners how to prepare soil, plant seeds, and harvest the crop. There were garden-tips film shows at the cinema and children's books with titles such as "Happy Hours on the Home Front". The BBC had a "Radio Allotment", a vegetable plot from which reports were broadcast weekly on the progress of 23 varieties of vegetables. More land was ploughed to boost farm production. Many young women joined the Women's Land Army as Land Girls, doing men's jobs on farms and in forestry.

DIG FOR VICTORY

▲ Posters like this one urged people to grow their own food. Magazine covers showed happy young women with pitchforks, rather than the elegant models of pre-war days.

▶ Newspaper photos showed cabbages flourishing on top of air raid shelters. There were vegetables in the dried-up moat of the Tower of London (pictured here), and pigs in the drained swimming pool of a smart London club.

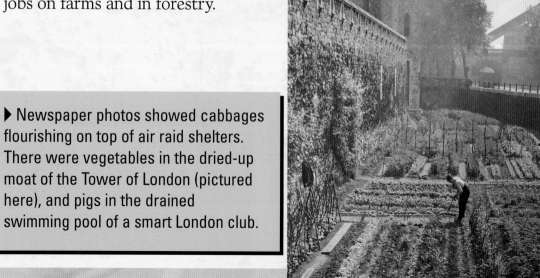

Eyewitness

Land Girl Doreen Godfrey joined the Women's Land Army at 17, in 1941. In 1942 she was shot at by a German plane while out in the fields with a horse and cart feeding maize leaves to cattle. She was hit in the foot and had to wear a plaster cast for a year. "Veteran" land girls passed on tips to newcomers – such as how to repair leaky shoes with melted beeswax and castor oil. A bicycle was useful too, since many girls were sent to remote farms, with no buses for miles.

▲ The Dig for Victory campaign was also popular in the United States, where children were encouraged to start "victory gardens".

◄ Land Girls gathering corn on a farm in southern England, 1944. Many Land Girls learned to handle tractors as well as horses.

The Land Girls

- The Women's Land Army (WLA) was started in World War I (1914–1918).

- It was re-formed in July 1939.

- Numbers of Land Girls rose from 7,000 in 1940 to over 80,000 in 1945.

- Land Girls were paid 32 shillings a week – about £1.60.

MAKE DO AND MEND

People were urged not to waste food or precious materials. "Make Do and Mend" meant not throwing away anything that could be recycled (used again).

Before the war, Britain had relied on ships to bring in much of its fuel, factory materials, and food (such as wheat). Now, however, German submarines were sinking hundreds of Allied ships crossing the Atlantic with supplies from the United States and **Commonwealth**. To save materials, such as cloth and metal, people were encouraged to recycle them.

Make your own clothes

From 1942, top fashion designers were asked to design "utility clothes" for factories to make cheaply. Many people made their own clothes: turning a blanket into a coat for instance. Women and children knitted woolly hats, gloves, and scarves. American families sent "clothes bundles" to Britain.

Salvage = recycling

"Salvage" meant recycling. Children collected old saucepans and scrap metal because the government told people that 15 tonnes of scrap meant one new tank. Iron railings from parks and gardens were melted down. People handed in rubber boots, toys, tyres, and beach rings so the rubber could be reused. Meat bones were turned into glue and explosives. Waste paper was recycled and envelopes were reused.

▶ This US poster urged Americans to salvage scrap metal in order to help their country's armed forces defeat the Japanese.

8 January 1940	January 1942	February 1942
Food rationing begins in Britain. Everyone is given a ration book. In June 1941, clothes are also rationed.	Tyres are rationed in the United States. The US Army needs them for jeeps, tractors, and aeroplanes.	Australia rations food and clothes. Meat rationing, Australians are told, means more food for Britain.

Clothes rationing

Clothes rationing began in Britain in June 1941:

- Leather, wool, cotton, and flax (for linen) were all in short supply.

- Customers had to use coupons with "points" at the shops.

- To buy a coat, a woman needed to hand over 15 points.

- For a child's dress, she needed 8 points.

- By early 1943, the clothes ration for one person for a year was just 48 points.

In the News

"The people of this country can congratulate themselves ... in the first twelve months more than a quarter of a million tons of shipping were saved in textiles alone. Nearly four hundred thousand men and women have been released from making cloth and clothing for civilians and have gone into the Services or to war production ... "
Hugh Dalton, British government minister for trade, was pleased with the success of clothes rationing.

◀ Utility clothes were designed to look stylish, but were made cheaply in factories using whatever materials were available.

21

March 1942
Germans suffer food shortages. By 1944, bread is severely rationed.

May 1942
Petrol is rationed in the eastern United States, and nationwide by December. Coffee is rationed by the end of the year, too.

April 1943
Meat, fats, canned food, and cheese are rationed in the United States. Wages are frozen, to stop prices rising.

Coping with rationing

Rationing food made sure that basic foods were shared equally and not wasted. Governments controlled the sale of meat, eggs, sugar, and other foods. Cooks were encouraged to make the best use of foods that were plentiful by trying recipes from books such as *Meals without Meat, Try Cooking Cabbage This Way*, and *Potato Pete's Recipe Book*.

No bananas, but no obesity

A song from 1943 had the wistful title *When Can I have a Banana Again?* Imported foods such as bananas and oranges became luxuries. People ate less, but most kept slim and healthy. People doing heavy work and soldiers got extra rations. Free orange juice and cod-liver oil for babies meant that many poorer children in Britain actually ate better because of rationing. Elsewhere, in Russia, China, and in the Netherlands in 1944–1945, food shortages meant that many people starved.

Food rations

In Britain in 1941, the weekly food ration per person included:

Tea	57g (2oz)
Butter or margarine	170g (6oz)
Jam or honey	227g (8oz)
Sugar	227g (8oz)
Cheese	57g (2oz)
Bacon	115g (4oz)
Milk	1.4 litres (3 pints)
Sweets (from July 1942)	85g (3oz)

The black market

By 1943, the British government reckoned that 700,000 ration books had been lost or stolen. Illegal trade, known as the black market, flourished. Criminals sold stolen goods while dishonest shopkeepers sold rationed goods "under the counter" (illegally).

▶ Every person was given a ration book. You could buy only a limited amount of each rationed food a week.

MAKE DO AND MEND

▶ Children in Britain enjoyed food sent from the United States, such as tins of Spam and fresh eggs, supplied under the Lend-Lease programme.

New foods and recipes

- Wartime dinners included such unfamiliar dishes as "parsnip, carrot, and potato pie".

- Dried egg powder made reasonable scrambled eggs.

- Whale meat went on sale in Britain.

- Germans made a sauce from beech nuts, salt, and an onion, to pour over potatoes.

- They also made "ersatz" coffee from acorns.

◀ A wartime cook made do with whatever was in the shops or could be found locally. "Have you tried young stinging nettles boiled as a vegetable?" was one suggestion.

FAMILY LIFE

It was difficult to have a normal family life. Many families were split by the war. Men and women were away in the armed forces or doing war work. Many who left home never returned.

Millions of people were in the services – the army, navy, and air force. For many, "joining up" soon meant going overseas to fight. At home, many women took full-time jobs, and this meant leaving the family for the first time. Before the war, grown-up sons and daughters had usually lived at home until they got married. Now many were leaving home by the age of 18.

Eyewitness

"I was married in 1943. Everyone in the village helped ... people gave me fat, sugar, fruit and eggs, and the baker made us a wedding cake. I wore a grey suit, white silk blouse and navy blue hat and shoes ... bought with coupons saved up for over one year."

A war bride remembers her wedding in June 1943. Quoted in The Home Front *(1981).*

▶ Many couples married, in spite of rationing and dangers. Newlyweds were often parted, but hoped to build new lives together when peace came.

September 1939	October 1940	January 1942
Australia, Canada, and India join the war on Britain's side. Men and women from these countries enrol for war service. Many come to Britain.	The United States calls up men for military service – the first peacetime compulsory draft in US history.	First US troops or "GIs" arrive in the United Kingdom, in Northern Ireland. Thousands of Americans are soon based in Britain, North Africa, and Australia.

◀ Railway stations were the scenes of tearful farewells as families were parted and men were waved off to war.

Separations and new responsibilities

Thousands of mothers said goodbye to their children in 1939, when city children were evacuated. For some, this separation lasted years. With so many men away, lots of children grew up without seeing much of their fathers. Servicemen came home only for brief rest-periods or "leaves". Those overseas were away for many months. Men who were captured by the enemy and held as prisoners of war were not seen by their families for up to five years. Children and parents had to get to know one another again, when families were reunited in 1945.

In wartime, older children grew up fast. They helped look after the home, and cared for younger brothers and sisters. Families who had been "bombed out" during the Blitz went to stay with relatives or friends. There was a lot of upheaval and moving around.

The worries of war

Wartime life was tiring and stressful. People did not get proper sleep, because of air raids. They spent hours on slow journeys by train or bus, and waiting in queues outside shops. Yet they had to work very hard. And every family dreaded the news that a relative or friend was missing, "presumed killed", or "killed in action".

December 1942	Spring 1943	1944–1945
Sir William Beveridge announces plans for a "welfare state" with free schools and health care in Britain after the war.	All women in Britain aged 18–45 must register for part-time or full-time war work.	More than 15 million Americans are in the armed forces. Not until after May 1945 do Allied troops start to come home.

Keeping in touch

During World War II, millions of people travelled far from home, often for the first time in their lives. Before the war, only the wealthy had travelled abroad for holidays.

Meeting the world

The Allied forces were huge and multi-national. Among the men and women in uniform were British, Americans, French, Poles, Australians, New Zealanders, Canadians, South Africans, Indians, West Indians, and many more. US troops arriving in Britain were warned that wartime Britain was different to home. And most British people knew about America only from films. Before 1942, few had ever met an American. They were surprised to learn that blacks and whites did not serve in the same units in the US Army.

The war brought new experiences and new friends, and strangers quickly became pals. Most Americans and British got on well and many friendships were made. Many wartime friendships endured for life.

In the News

"If you expect white cliffs and thatched cottages, you will be disappointed ... The people will be glad to see you but their enthusiasm is usually of a rather quiet sort."

Extract from a leaflet welcoming US servicemen to Britain in 1942

Eyewitness

Some words in American English were not the same as in British English, as Robert Arbid, an American soldier, discovered. He told a British magazine in 1944:

"We were amazed to find that people [in England] used their own peculiar language ... new to our ears!"

▲ A wartime **telegram** was seldom good news. A brief official message usually told the reader that a relative was missing in action or dead.

Welcome letters

Letters, rather than phone calls, kept families in touch. Troops overseas waited expectantly for the next mail sack, hoping for letters from wives, girlfriends, or parents. Birthday and Christmas cards were smaller than in peacetime, but still treasured. So were family photos, perhaps showing a baby that an absent father had not yet seen.

▶ Soldiers' letters were read by a **censor**. The censor crossed or cut out anything he or she thought might help the enemy — such as "I am leaving for India today", or "we have just been given new rifles".

◀ A US soldier in 1945 said "We have learned in the years of being away from home that mail from our families and friends is the thing that kept us going in spirit."

A CHANGED WORLD

A CHANGED WORLD

In 1945, people in the Allied nations celebrated victory, with parades and street parties. When the victory parties were over, the post-war world presented new challenges.

People remembered the comradeship shared on the Home Front. They recalled funny moments, but seldom spoke about the fear, hardship, and sadness. The war was enormously costly. Nearly everyone had lost a friend or a relative. Across much of Europe and Asia, towns and villages were in ruins, industries were shattered, and roads, ports, and railways were wrecked. There was a huge rebuilding task ahead.

Hopes for a new world

After six years of war, people were exhausted but looked forward to a brighter future. During the battle against bombs, shortages, and blackouts, they had hung on in the hope of victory and peace. Most of the **Allies** believed the war had been right, to defeat evil and make sure that nothing like the Holocaust should ever happen again. Germany and Japan were occupied by the Allies. They faced years of reconstruction, but even in the defeated countries most people were relieved the war was over.

In 1945 millions of servicemen handed in their uniforms and weapons, and returned to civilian life. As they planned for the future, people rebuilt their homes and picked up the pieces of family life. Some went back to their old jobs; others had fresh plans now there was peace.

▶ People all over the world celebrated victory with street parties and parades. These revellers in New York are rejoicing on Victory in Europe Day (VE Day), 8 May 1945.

TIMELINE

1939
1 June Women's Land Army is re-formed in Britain.
1 September Germany invades Poland. World War II begins.
3 September Britain and France declare war on Germany. Evacuation of children from British cities has already begun.

1940
January Food rationing begins in Britain.
April Germany invades Denmark and Norway.
May Germany invades Belgium, the Netherlands, and France.
30 June Germany invades the Channel Islands.
June US government tells all foreigners they must register with the Federal authorities because it is concerned they might be a threat to security.
July Britain is threatened by a German invasion.
September The Blitz on British towns and cities begins. Women serve as air raid precaution (ARP) wardens, ambulance drivers, and voluntary helpers.
14 November German planes bomb Coventry.

1941
March British government takes new powers to order people to do war work. People are asked not to use buses and trains after 4 p.m., so workers can get home.
April Germany and its allies invade Greece and Yugoslavia.
May Worst Blitz raids on London.
June Germany and its allies invade the Soviet Union.
June Clothes rationing begins in Britain.

July Coal is rationed in Britain.
7 December Japanese attack on Pearl Harbor brings the United States into the war.
8 December Britain and Canada declare war on Japan.

1942
January US government puts Japanese-Americans in special camps because it thinks they might help Japan in the war.
February Japanese forces are very near Australia. Australia's prime minister, John Curtin, announces food rationing.
March Introduction of utility clothing in Britain.
May Start of petrol rationing in the United States.
June Last Jewish schools in Germany are closed by the Nazis.
July Sweets are rationed in Britain.
October US government "freezes" wages, rents, and prices.

1943
February Allies begin bombing Germany night and day.
February A German army surrenders at Stalingrad, ending German advance into the USSR.
April Some foods, including meat, are rationed in the United States. Around this time, all women in Britain aged 18–45 must register for war work.
May The Warsaw Rising of Polish resistance fighters is crushed.
July Allies land in Sicily, to begin the invasion of Italy.

1944
January British government passes a new Education Act, planning post-war education.

April Very heavy Allied air attacks on German cities.
April Britain's first prefabricated home is shown to the public – the two-bedroom homes will be built in sections in factories.
April Much of southern England is a huge military camp, in preparation for the invasion of Europe.
6 June D-Day; Allied armies invade France to begin the liberation of France.
13 June First German V-1 flying bomb falls on London.
September Streetlights turned on in Britain as the blackout is eased. V-2 attacks begin.
September Allies enter Germany. Nazis form their own "Home Guard", called the *Volkssturm*.
October German bread ration is cut to one loaf a week.

1945
14 February Allied bombers destroy Dresden in Germany.
12 April Death of US President F. D. Roosevelt. Harry S Truman becomes president.
30 April Hitler kills himself as Soviet armies close in on Berlin.
2 May Berlin is captured by the Allies.
7 May Germany surrenders.
8 May (VE (Victory in Europe) Day. End of the war in Europe.
6 August Allies drop an atomic bomb on Japanese city of Hiroshima and another on Nagasaki three days later. Japan surrenders.
14 August V-J Day (Victory over Japan) ends the war.

GLOSSARY

air raid attack on a target by aircraft dropping bombs

Allies nations that fought against Germany, Japan, and Italy during World War II

blackout measures to reduce all lights showing at night, to hide possible targets from enemy bombers

Blitz short for *Blitzkrieg*, German for "lightning war". The term "Blitz" is used to describe the German bombing of Britain, beginning in 1940.

casualties people injured or killed during a war

censor official who read letters and newspaper articles, taking out any information useful to an enemy

civilian someone who is not in the armed forces

collaborators people who cooperate with an enemy that has taken over their country

Commonwealth countries formerly part of the British Empire

death-camps Nazi prison camps where Jews and other people were gassed to death

evacuate move people from danger to safer places

ghetto area of a city within which Jews were confined

Holocaust mass killing of Jews and others by the Nazis during World War II

identity card card showing a person's photo and personal details

Nazi member of the National Socialist German Workers' Party, led by Adolf Hitler

occupation when a country is invaded and ruled by another country

patriotic loving and supporting one's own country

propaganda control of information in the media to show your own side in a good light

Resistance groups of people who fought against enemy forces occupying their country

sabotage break equipment or slow down work in a factory, or damage railway lines, bridges, and telephone wires to hinder an enemy

sandbags bags filled with earth or sand to protect buildings and people from bomb damage

Special Operations Executive (SOE) British organization that sent secret agents to help the Resistance in France and other occupied countries

telegram message sent by phone for speed, but delivered as a short printed message

FINDING OUT MORE

If you are interested in finding out more about World War II, here are some more books and websites you might find useful.

Further reading

Your local public library's adult section should have plenty of war books, including books about what it was like to live on the home front. Written by people who were actually there, such books will give you an idea of what ordinary people thought about the war and their part in it.

Books for younger readers

Britain at War: Air Raids, Martin Parson (Wayland, 1999)

Causes and Consequences of the Second World War, Stewart Ross (Evans, 2003)

Causes of World War II, Paul Dowswell (Heinemann Library, 2002)

History Through Poetry; World War II, Reg Grant (Hodder Wayland, 2001)

Hunger in Holland: Life during the Nazi Occupation, Cornelia Fuykschot (Prometheus Books, 1995)

World in Flames: In the Air, Peter Hepplewhite (Macmillan Children's Books, 2001)

World in Flames: On Land, Neil Tonge (Macmillan Children's Books, 2001)

WW2 Stories: War at Home, Anthony Masters (Franklin Watts, 2004)

WW2 Stories: War in the Air, Anthony Masters (Franklin Watts, 2004)

WW2 True Stories, Clive Gifford (Hodder Children's Books, 2002)

Websites

http://www.iwm.org.uk/ – the website of the Imperial War Museum in London.

http://www.wartimememories.co.uk/ – a website containing wartime recollections, including those of people who experienced life on the home front.

http://bbc.co.uk/history/war/wwtwo/ – this website from the BBC has lots of resources about World War II.

INDEX